ROSALIND
FRANKLIN
DNA DISCOVERER

By Tom Streissguth

Content Consultant
Dr. Amy Bix
Professor of History
Iowa State University

Essential Library
An Imprint of Abdo Publishing | abdopublishing.com

ABDOPUBLISHING.COM

Published by Abdo Publishing, a division of ABDO, PO Box 398166, Minneapolis, Minnesota 55439. Copyright © 2018 by Abdo Consulting Group, Inc. International copyrights reserved in all countries. No part of this book may be reproduced in any form without written permission from the publisher. Essential Library™ is a trademark and logo of Abdo Publishing.

Printed in the United States of America, North Mankato, Minnesota
042017
092017

Cover Photo: Jewish Chronicle/Heritage Images/Glow Images
Interior Photos: World History Archive/Alamy, 4, 17; Photo 51 by Rosalind Franklin and Raymond Gosling, 1952, courtesy of King's College London, 11; Science Source, 12, 38, 47, 48, 70, 76; AP Images, 15, 18; Everett Historical/Shutterstock Images, 20, 36; Edwin Dwight Babbitt/Internet Archive Book Images, 23; War Posters/Alamy, 27; iStockphoto, 30, 57; J. Wildman/iStockphoto, 44; Shutterstock Images, 51; King's College London Archives/Science Source, 53, 58, 60; Anthony Camerano/AP Images, 54; Photo Researchers Inc/Alamy, 62; A. Barrington Brown/Science Source, 68; Martin Shields/Science Source, 73; PA Images/Alamy, 82; Jewish Chronicle/Heritage Images/Glow Images, 84; A. Barry Dowsett/Science Source, 87; Peter J. Carroll/AP Images, 88; Steve Gschmeissner/Science Source, 90; David Pearson/Alamy, 95; Blend Images/Shutterstock Images, 96

Editor: Amanda Lanser
Series Designer: Nikki Farinella

PUBLISHER'S CATALOGING–IN–PUBLICATION DATA

Names: Streissguth, Tom, author.
Title: Rosalind Franklin: DNA discoverer / by Tom Streissguth.
Other titles: DNA discoverer
Description: Minneapolis, MN : Abdo Publishing, 2018. | Series: Women in
    science | Includes bibliographical references and index.
Identifiers: LCCN 2016962269 | ISBN 9781532110429 (lib. bdg.) |
    ISBN 9781680788273 (ebook)
Subjects: LCSH: Franklin, Rosalind, 1920-1958--Juvenile literature. | Women
    molecular biologists--Great Britain--Biography--Juvenile literature. | DNA--
    History--Juvenile literature.
Classification: DDC 572.8/092 [B]--dc23
LC record available at http://lccn.loc.gov/2016962269

CONTENTS

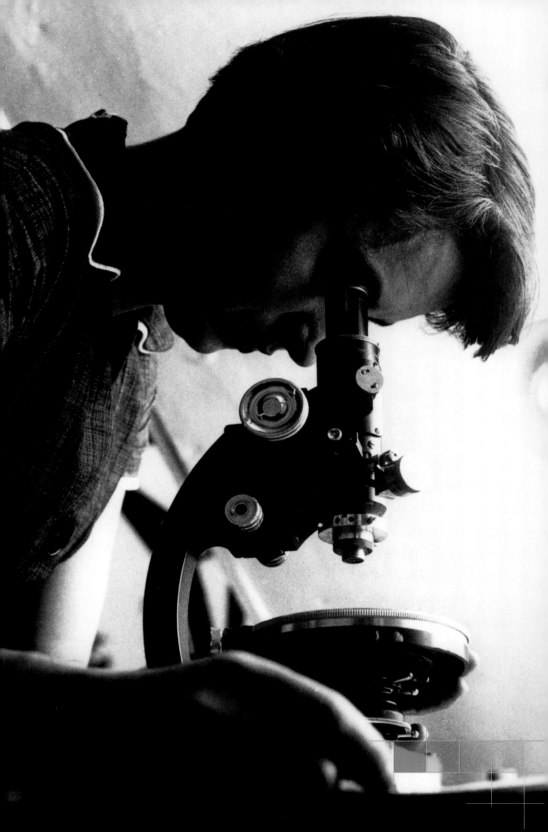

PHOTOGRAPH 51

It was May 1952, in London, England. The spring days brought welcome sunshine after the long and dreary English winter. But on other days, thick clouds of what Britons called London fog descended on the city, coating sidewalks, streets, and buildings with grime. This fog was a swirling, thick soup of coal smoke, factory emissions, and toxic chemicals. But Rosalind Franklin barely noticed.

Throughout the spring of 1952, Franklin and her student and laboratory partner, Raymond Gosling, spent long hours indoors. They worked with temperamental cameras and complicated X-ray machines. Their damp basement lab at King's College was in an old house with narrow staircases, thin walls, and a leaky roof. Franklin and Gosling's experiments could be frustrating,

Rosalind Franklin hard at work in her lab, where she was one of just a handful of female scientists

and the math they had to use was complex. Yet the work was leading them on a trail of discovery into the fundamental secrets of life.

Women in Chemistry

Women have made important contributions to chemistry since the science began. In the late eighteenth century, Marie Lavoisier worked as a laboratory assistant to her husband, Antoine-Laurent, helping him develop a new scientific method for understanding the elements. She translated scientific articles from English to French and created beautifully precise drawings of laboratory experiments and equipment.

Born in Poland, Marie Curie worked as a researcher in physics and chemistry in France. With her husband, Pierre, Curie discovered the elements polonium and radium. Their studies of radioactivity earned the two a share of the 1903 Nobel Prize in physics. After Pierre's death, Marie helped develop the medical use of X rays and won the 1911 Nobel Prize in chemistry, making her the first person ever to earn two Nobel Prizes. Dorothy Hodgkin, like Rosalind Franklin, was a skilled X-ray crystallographer. Using this method, she discovered the structure of penicillin, insulin, and vitamin B12. She won a Nobel Prize for her work in chemistry in 1964.

THE DOUBLE HELIX

Franklin and Gosling were creating X-ray images of thin, delicate, fiber-like structures. By measuring the details on the image, they could figure out how chemical compounds and molecules—invisible even to microscopes—made up the structures. One image, taken by Gosling, showed two strands crossing each other in the shape of an X. The strands appeared as a series of steps, like the rungs of two ladders crossing in the center. Franklin and Gosling were not sure what to make of the image, but the shape of the strands was clear: they showed the structure of a double helix. The image was much sharper than many others the scientists had taken in the lab. It became known as *Photograph 51*.

Franklin was secretive about her work, as were other scientists working in the lab. They wanted the opportunity to announce discoveries as their own. Instead of showing the image to her colleagues, she kept it with other images in her office. When she was ready with her calculations and findings, she would write everything in a paper. She would share the paper with a few other scientists at King's College. Then she would announce her findings at a lecture or seminar. She would seek input from her scientific peers and then prepare an article for publication in a journal. This would allow her to claim a discovery—if, in fact, the photograph showed anything significant.

Gosling and Franklin were also competing with other scientists in England and in the United States. In fact, James Watson and Francis Crick, members of the prestigious Cavendish Laboratory at Cambridge University, were working on the same problem: the structure of deoxyribonucleic acid, or DNA for short, the molecule that passes genetic information from parents to offspring. Linus Pauling, a molecular chemist at the California Institute of Technology, was publishing articles on this very subject, and he was drawing near to a solution

Secrets of *Photograph 51*

For such an important image in the history of science, *Photograph 51* does not look like much—only a blurry image of two broken lines crossing at the center to form an X. But the image shows several important facts. The X pattern is created by a helical molecule, which appears in the image as two branches crossing at perpendicular angles. Four white diamond shapes, at top, bottom, left and right, indicate the helix pattern continues repeating itself beyond the image boundaries. In addition, the top and bottom diamonds are slightly lighter, which means the backbones of the molecule lie on the outside of the molecule and the chemical bases on the inside.

that every scientist in the same field knew would bring honors and fame.

It was not only the math, the use of complicated equipment, and the competition that were challenging Franklin. Every other researcher at King's College, and nearly all of the scientists at the Cavendish Laboratory, were men. Although they respected her ability, they did not completely accept her as a colleague. She did not take part in the casual, friendly conversations in which ideas could be traded and solutions challenged. She could not eat at the exclusively male college dining halls or relax at the men-only British pubs.

Nevertheless, Franklin was closing in on a solution to one of the most important scientific mysteries: how an organism passes its structure and characteristics to the next generation. Although her training was in chemistry, this work was bringing her into new realms of genetics and molecular biology. Her discoveries would eventually bring her renown as one of the most talented

SCIENCE
SPOTLIGHT

THE DISCOVERY OF DNA

In 1869, young German researcher Johann Friedrich Miescher made an interesting discovery. Miescher wanted to study what was inside a single cell. First, he collected pus from a hospital's used bandages. He created tiny samples to look at the cells that made up the pus. Through a series of experiments, Miescher managed to extract a new chemical from the cells. Because this material came from the cell nucleus, he called it nuclein. Hydrogen, oxygen, nitrogen, and phosphorous atoms were present in nuclein, which made it a relatively simple molecule.

In Miescher's time, there were many theories afloat on the mechanism of heredity. How do parents pass on their characteristics to offspring? Why do people have blue, brown, and hazel eyes, for example, and how does this single trait—one among many—come about in a newborn? The botanist Gregor Mendel, in his study of pea plants, concluded that both parents pass on a set of instructions to their offspring and that certain traits are dominant—more likely to appear in a younger generation. But the mechanism of passing on the genetic map was still unknown. Miescher and other scientists realized that some component of the human cell must be responsible. But in Miescher's view, nuclein's simple chemistry disqualified it from having anything to do with the complex way humans inherit characteristics from their parents. Eventually, in the 1930s, nuclein would gain a new, more precise name: deoxyribonucleic acid, or DNA.

scientific researchers of the twentieth century. But in the early 1950s, she had to follow where opportunities led. The grants and stipends that supported her work came from institutions that were pursuing scientific problems of their own, and these did not necessarily match her interests. As an independent woman who needed to support herself, she had to consider carefully any opportunities that came her way.

She still was not sure about the significance of *Photograph 51*. In her view, the molecule's structure needed to be worked out precisely, using careful mathematical calculations and relying on evidence and proven facts. A simple photograph, a theory, or even a three-dimensional model simply was not enough. DNA, the chemical code of life, was too important to be solved with such pictures and toys. It had to be solved the right way—the scientific way.

Photograph 51

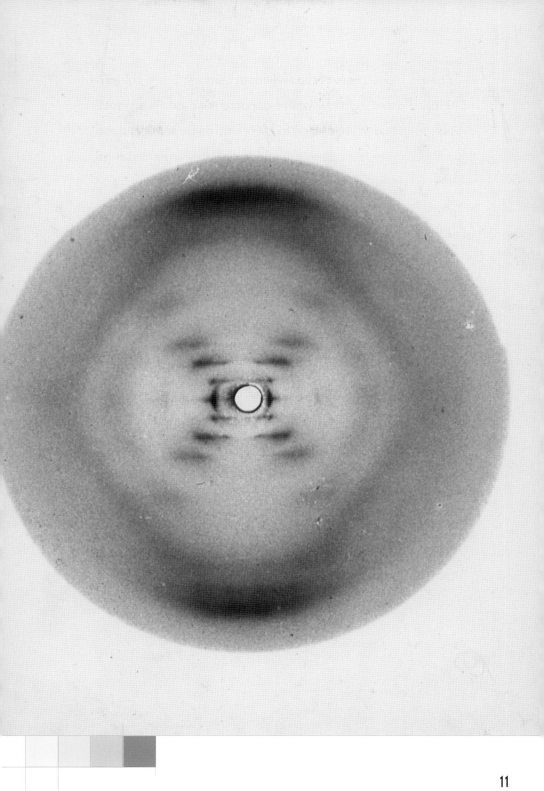

TWO

GROWING UP SMART

The Franklins, a middle-class Jewish family, lived in a comfortable London neighborhood. Ellis Franklin was a banker and part owner of Routledge & Kegan Paul, a publishing company. On July 25, 1920, Muriel and Ellis Franklin's second child, Rosalind, was born.

Ellis was a busy and ambitious man. He strived for success in business. He also volunteered his time to worthy causes. Ellis believed in the value of a quality education. He pushed Rosalind and her four siblings to do well in school. He expected his sons to follow him into banking. He wanted his daughters to become capable, happy housewives.

Rosalind in Norway in approximately 1940

But even from a young age, Rosalind's future seemed likely to include achievements beyond the home. Rosalind did not need much encouragement in school. She was an eager learner and an exceptional math student. She found it easy to learn new languages, but science courses fascinated her most of all. Ellis sent her to Saint Paul's Girls' School, one of a very few English schools that offered advanced science courses to young women.

Saint Paul's was a day school in West London, famous for its difficult classes and the philosophy that young girls should train for future careers beyond motherhood and keeping a home. Every morning, Rosalind put on the blue uniform and blue felt hat that marked a Saint Paul's student, known affectionately as a Paulina, and took a bus to the school. She studied math, geography, Latin, French, and science; took part in sports including cricket and tennis; and made several close friends.

Alma Mater

The Saint Paul's Girls' School opened its doors in 1904 at Brook Green, London. The science block, where Rosalind first studied chemistry and physics, was founded in 1933. Saint Paul's Girls' School had a great hall for concerts and a music wing, and it was the only girls' school in the United Kingdom at the time to have an indoor swimming pool.

CONFLICT IN EUROPE

Rosalind's life in London was a happy one. But in Europe, trouble was brewing. In early 1933, Adolf Hitler came to power in Germany. Hitler was the head of the National Socialist, or Nazi, Party. He

Jewish refugees from Germany receive a warm meal in England in 1938.

promised to solve many of Germany's problems, including high unemployment and social turmoil. He scapegoated Germany's Jewish population, blaming them and their non-Jewish supporters for all the country's problems.

Sensing dangerous times ahead, many Jewish families fled Germany. Ellis believed helping these families was his duty. He and Rosalind volunteered at Woburn House, where they helped Jewish refugees find housing and employment. Working with the British government, Ellis also arranged entry permits for refugees and helped find homes for Jewish orphans. The Franklins even took two young Austrian refugees into their home in London.

AT CAMBRIDGE

Upon graduating from Saint Paul's in 1938, Rosalind was one of four students who won an annual stipend of £30 a year for outstanding work in her classes.[1] This award was intended to help students pay for tuition and expenses for university studies.

Rosalind's excellent grades earned her a place at Newnham College at Cambridge University. Newnham was the prestigious school's women's college. She took rigorous classes in physics and chemistry as well as languages, including French. When it was time to select a major, she chose physical chemistry.

There were well-equipped labs and highly qualified teachers at Cambridge. The school's Cavendish Laboratory was one of the leading research laboratories in the world. But not long after Rosalind began her studies, World War II

Rosalind's Bookshelf

While at Saint Paul's Girls' School, Rosalind earned high grades in science and won several prizes. One of these awards offered her a book of her choice. She selected *New Pathways in Science* by Arthur Eddington, a book that discussed theories of subatomic structure and the strange, new field of quantum mechanics. Even for a successful student at Saint Paul's Girls' School, it was an ambitious choice: Rosalind was only 15 years old at the time she requested the book.

In 1940, war threatened Rosalind's future career as a researcher.

(1939–1945) broke out in Europe. In September 1939, Hitler's Germany invaded its neighbor, Poland, without provocation. Poland was an ally of the United Kingdom. The British government immediately declared war on Germany. Many scientists in the United Kingdom left their laboratories for new jobs in the war effort. Other scientists, many of them German, lost their jobs. The British government arrested some of them as suspected spies and enemy agents.

The war spread to the rest of Europe in 1940. The German army marched into France and seized Paris, the country's capital. French refugees streamed out of the country, some of them immigrating to the United Kingdom. One of them was Adrienne Weill. Weill arrived at Cambridge after the fall of Paris. She was a metallurgist who studied the chemical properties of metals. Weill gave Rosalind private lessons in French and soon became her friend and mentor. She would inspire Rosalind to become a professional scientific researcher.

British troops wait to board a train to join the fighting in France in 1939.

CHAPTER
THREE

WAR YEARS

A fter its successful invasion of Poland, the German army rolled across Western Europe. Belgium, the Netherlands, and France all fell to Nazi tanks and infantry in the spring of 1940. Germany occupied Paris and set up a puppet government led by French officials who were under German control. As the continent fell to Adolf Hitler and the Nazis, the British soon understood they were in for a long war.

In 1940, Germany also began its campaign against the British Isles. German planes rained down bombs on London and industrial cities, such as Birmingham and Coventry, in England. Fire spread through the streets, destroying buildings and killing hundreds of people. Franklin, still studying in Cambridge, was also in the line of fire. Home to a prestigious university,

Approximately 1.5 million German troops invaded Poland along the country's entire border with Germany.

Cambridge was not a military target. Nevertheless, Germany staged several air raids on the city.

Undeterred by the air raids, Franklin and her fellow students continued their work in the university's research laboratories. Franklin had won a research fellowship to continue working under the guidance of chemistry professor Ronald George Wreyford Norrish. He was studying the effect light energy has on a substance's chemical makeup. When a substance is exposed to light, its chemistry can change. The atoms and molecules rearrange themselves, forming new structures. A familiar example is the exposure of sensitive film to light, creating a photograph.

Part of this transformation is a change in energy. When an atom or molecule changes from a high energy state to a low energy state, it emits radiation in the form of light. Different wavelengths of visible light

Jocelyn Bell Burnell

Susan Jocelyn Bell, later Jocelyn Bell Burnell, also studied at Cambridge University. She helped build a radio telescope, an instrument that searches the outermost limits of the universe by detecting radio waves. While searching the sky in 1967, Bell came across a strange, rapidly repeating signal. When she told her fellow scientists, they said it must be a malfunction of the scope or she was misreading the data. But the signal continued, and Bell eventually proved it came from a distant, rapidly rotating star called a pulsar.

This discovery was hailed as one of the most important astronomical discoveries of the twentieth century. But Bell was not recognized for her work. Instead, the Nobel Prize for her discovery was awarded to a colleague and her supervisor at Cambridge, both men.

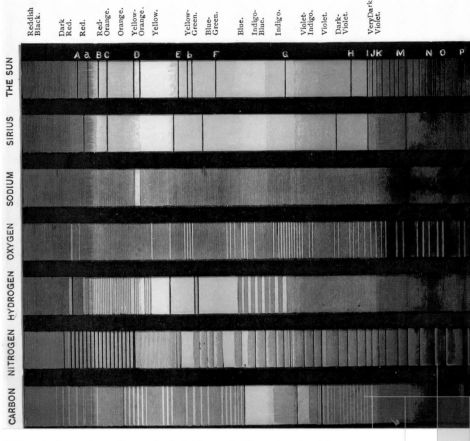

Different elements on the periodic table emit different parts of the light spectrum.

create a wide range of colors, called a spectrum. The pattern of these colors is unique to each element and compound. Examining the spectrum of a substance gives important clues to its underlying structure.

To explore this phenomenon, Norrish built a powerful lamp that emitted light pulses in short bursts toward a substance. After the exposure, he examined the spectrum of colors emitted by the substance to understand how its chemistry had changed.

Norrish, however, was a difficult man to work with. He was ill-tempered and accepted no challenge or disagreement from those working under his guidance. Nor did Norrish think much of a woman aspiring to scientific achievement. He gave Franklin cramped and dark rooms to work in and trivial chemistry problems to solve. When she pointed out a mistake in one of his theorems, the two had a bitter argument. In a letter home, Franklin explained her relationship with her advisor, writing, "He's the sort of person who likes you all right as long as you say yes to everything he says, and agree with all his mis-statements, and I always refuse to do that."[1]

Though work was stressful, Franklin was able to relax at the hostel where she lived. Invited there by Weill, the hostel was home to many foreign students who shared living space. In the evenings, Franklin enjoyed speaking foreign languages or talking science with her mentor. In 1941, Franklin completed undergraduate courses and had done the work to earn a bachelor's degree. But because Cambridge University policy forbade Franklin and other female students from being awarded degrees, she did not receive her degree until the policy changed in 1947. The difficult courses in chemistry, math, and physics were finally over. But Franklin wanted to spend her career as a scientist. She would need a more advanced degree.

A DIFFICULT DECISION

Before she could continue her studies, Franklin needed to make a difficult decision. Her country was at war. She had to decide whether she would contribute to the war effort or continue her studies to earn her doctor of philosophy, or PhD, degree. Franklin found a way to do both.

Women Join the War Effort

The British war effort involved every citizen. Starting in 1941, Franklin and all other British women between the ages of 18 and 60 years had to register with the government. The National Service Act, passed in December 1941, made all unmarried women between ages 20 and 30 eligible for military service. All female research students at Cambridge and elsewhere had to be "de-reserved," meaning available for work directly connected with the war effort.[2] Male researchers, on the other hand, could remain reserved as researchers, if they so chose.

Franklin had a difficult decision to make—whether to apply for reserved status or make herself available for any war-work assignment that might come her way. Eventually she accepted a position at the British Coal Utilisation Research Association (BCURA). Other women became air raid wardens, served as nurses, or held positions in government and military offices. The Women's Voluntary Service (WVS) and the Auxiliary Territorial Service trained women to aim antiaircraft guns, operate searchlights, and put out fires on pump crews. Women served as codebreakers, and some parachuted into enemy territory to sabotage German military installations, deliver secret communications, and operate radios. The WVS became the Women's Royal Voluntary Service in 1966 and is still active today.

In 1941, the war was not going well for the United Kingdom and its allies. Germany controlled much of Europe and had invaded parts of the Soviet Union. Franklin's father believed British citizens had the patriotic duty to fight Germany in any way possible. He had joined a government ministry that passed out small metal shelters that people placed in their homes to protect themselves from falling debris. Franklin's brothers had joined the military. Both of Franklin's parents wanted Rosalind to take part, too.

Franklin could have applied to work at various government ministries engaged in war work. Though important to the war effort, such a position would be uninteresting and not likely to create a lifelong career. It would also not contribute to her PhD.

Though she was as patriotic as the rest of her family, Franklin did not want to be shuffled into an uninteresting assignment. The best outcome would be to engage in research useful to the war effort that could later allow her to advance in her field. Such an opportunity arrived from an unexpected source.

HOLES IN COAL

In 1942, the British Coal Utilisation Research Association (BCURA) sent Franklin an interesting offer. If she left Cambridge for London, she could join BCURA as an assistant research officer. She would be investigating the molecular properties of coal—how it was built out of carbon atoms, why there were so many different kinds of it, how its chemistry and properties changed under heat and pressure. Such a project would allow Franklin to work on research she could turn into a doctoral thesis.

Coal was an important fuel for the Allied militaries and home front during World War II.

British Coal Research

Coal research continued to be critical after the war. The scientists at the BCURA lab still made discoveries, and the agency had chemistry, physics, and math departments working to uncover coal's many scientific secrets. There was a boiler department, a combustion department, and a department to test home appliances. But by the 1960s, the coal industry went into decline in the face of new energy technologies such as diesel and nuclear power. The government stopped funding for coal research. The BCURA lab closed permanently in 1972.

At the time, coal was a common heating fuel for homes and industry, but there were many properties of the dark black rock that scientists still did not understand. It was also an important war resource. Coal was needed to fuel warships and railroad locomotives. British cities depended on coal to generate electricity. Franklin realized her work at the BCURA lab could be useful to British manufacturers and the military. Returning to London would also bring her closer to family and friends. In the fall of 1942, Franklin prepared to leave Weill's hostel in Cambridge. She was moving to London to take up a new field of research: the holes in coal.

SCIENCE
SPOTLIGHT

SCIENCE IN WARTIME

The British war effort involved more than infantry troops, fighter aircraft, navy submarines, and ships and paratroopers. In addition to the armed forces, a corps of dedicated scientists worked hard to keep British military and defense technology ahead of Germany's. A team of codebreakers developed early programmable computers to crack the Enigma code, used by the Nazi government to transmit instructions to officers and spies. The mass production of the first antibiotic, penicillin, made it possible to treat dangerous infections such as gangrene, which threatened the limbs and lives of wounded soldiers.

The installation of new radar systems on the coast of England allowed British air defense systems to shoot down hundreds of German bombers before they reached cities such as London and Birmingham. British scientists saw radar's usefulness on the ground and in the air, where advanced night-vision radar scopes helped bomber pilots see their targets in all kinds of weather and at high altitude. British scientists also took part in the Manhattan Project, the effort by the United States to develop an atomic weapon. In this effort, the Allies were in a frantic race with Germany, where scientists working in secret laboratories and bunkers built the first long-range missiles designed to create panic and mass civilian casualties in British cities.

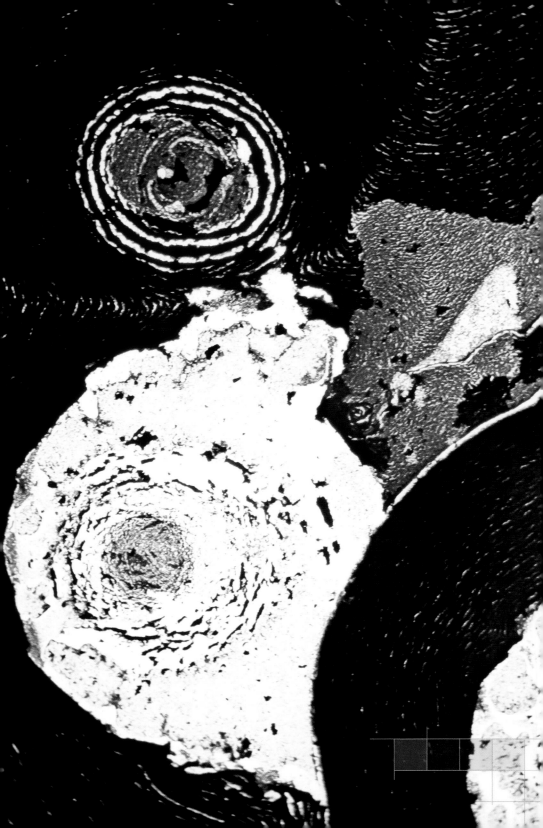

FOUR

STUDYING THE HOLES IN COAL

In 1942, Franklin began her coal research at the BCURA laboratory. Her task was to explore coal's porosity—its ability to hold gases and fluids under different conditions. The basic science question was to understand how the molecular structure of coal made it porous. Why were some kinds of coal more porous than others? How and why did the chemical structure change? And how could this knowledge aid the British military in the war effort?

There are different kinds of coal. Lignite, or brown coal, is a soft, crumbly material that burns with a smoky flame. It is not an efficient producer of heat, compared with bituminous coal, which is harder, darker, and more like rock. Anthracite is the highest grade of coal, a shiny black rock that burns efficiently.

Coal soot as seen under a microscope

Where Does Coal Come From?

Coal is a rock that is a product of dead plants buried underground and subjected to heat, pressure, and time. Over the course of millions of years, the decomposed plants are transformed into a flammable substance that is primarily carbon but also contains hydrogen, oxygen, and other elements. Humans living on the British Isles have used coal as a heating fuel since at least the time of the Roman Empire. During World War II, coal was an important fuel for the United Kingdom. But many coal miners were serving overseas in the military. In 1943, nearly 10 percent of the 18-year-old young men who were drafted to serve the country were assigned to mine coal.[1]

The higher the carbon content of coal, the higher its grade, and the more potential energy it stores.

In her research, Franklin compared the porosity of these different types of coal. She predicted that small structures in coal made it more or less porous. These structures, called micropores, were invisible, even through a microscope. Micropores had to be measured and analyzed by a chemist. Franklin would have to create a well-designed experiment and use logic, math, and her knowledge of chemistry and physics to study the micropores. The BCURA lab had up-to-date equipment, including an electron microscope, a device invented in 1931, that would help Franklin find the answers.

BUILDING AN EXPERIMENT

The BCURA lab collected coal samples from all over Britain. There were lignite, sub-bituminous, bituminous, and anthracite coal samples available for study. Franklin's first step was to grind her samples into a fine powder. Placing a single sample in a glass tube, she used a pump to create a vacuum in the tube. The vacuum eliminated all the air in the tube. The various gases in the air—nitrogen, oxygen, and carbon dioxide—would throw off her measurements.

Franklin's next step was to measure how different elements react with coal and how they are absorbed by coal. She introduced the elements, one by one, into the vial holding the coal powder, and then she measured the concentration of the materials that remained in the vacuum. She could then calculate how much of the material the coal had absorbed. Franklin found the most useful element in her experiment was helium gas, which has a simple atomic structure: two electrons orbiting a nucleus made of two protons and two neutrons. Franklin used other, more complex materials as well, including water, methanol, hexane, and benzene.

For months, Franklin designed, set up, and carried out hundreds of experimental measurements. Through her work, she gained a new, more complete understanding of coal's structure. Franklin had made an important discovery. Microstructures allowed a simple molecule such as helium to be absorbed into the coal, whereas other more complex molecules, such as hexane and benzene, could not pass through.

The microstructures acted like a sieve, letting the simpler elements combine with coal's carbon atoms.

During her experiment, Franklin took measurements at high temperatures to analyze the porosity of coal under heat. Franklin heated the samples to very high temperatures, up to 2,900 degrees Fahrenheit (1,600°C).[2] The high temperature caused a breakdown in the coal's chemical structure and changed its form, a process known as carbonization. As the coal grew hotter, its porosity increased. It absorbed other substances more easily. All of Franklin's results were carefully noted, and eventually the experiment would be written as a scientific paper.

THE WAR'S END

Franklin's work at BCURA was challenging and rewarding. It allowed a new classification system for different kinds of coal, which allowed British industries to use coal more efficiently in manufacturing and power generation. Through these discoveries, Franklin made an original and practical contribution to scientific knowledge. But her life was not all about the holes in coal. She escaped London to go on climbing vacations in Wales, scaling the highest and toughest mountains and braving fog and cold to reach their peaks.

Meanwhile, Europe was still embroiled in war. But the Allies were turning the tide in Europe. On June 6, 1944, a vast

The Holocaust, Genetics, and Eugenics

Before World War II, Germany had been a leader in the science of genetics, with many German scientists adopting the theories of American eugenicists. The field of eugenics was popular in the United States and Europe in the early twentieth century. Based on new research into heredity, scientists in this field developed ways to improve the human organism by eliminating certain unwanted characteristics, such as inherited illnesses and mental disabilities. Eugenicists believed the best method to achieve this was to prevent reproduction by people who carried undesirable traits. In the United States during the 1920s, there were calls to weed out what they believed were "lesser" or "weaker" groups, such as African Americans and certain ethnic immigrants, by sterilizing them, while encouraging "biologically stronger" couples to have more children.

Once the Nazi party came to power, many German scientists took these eugenic theories further down a dark path. The most famous of them was Josef Mengele, who worked at the Auschwitz concentration camp in occupied Poland. There, he conducted a series of cruel experiments on human prisoners without their consent. His experiments were meant to determine how and why inherited traits are passed from parents to children. Mengele considered himself a scientist first and foremost. But many of Mengele's experiments resulted in the deaths of his human subjects. He also participated in the selection of Jewish prisoners and others for execution in the gas chambers during the Holocaust.

army of American, Canadian, British, and Australian troops stormed the beaches of Normandy in northern France. The Allied armies pushed back the Germans from the coast. Hitler then deployed the weapon he believed would win the war for Germany. Self-propelling V-2 bombs appeared in the skies over London. They crashed into streets and houses with terrifying explosive force. As an air warden, Franklin walked the streets,

As an air warden, Franklin hoped to prevent destruction from happening in other parts of London.

watching for lights in windows that violated the rules by making it easier for German bomber pilots to see their targets from high altitudes.

In May 1945, Germany surrendered to the Allies. The United Kingdom had emerged from the war damaged but victorious. Rosalind Franklin had also won a victory. In 1945, Franklin completed her doctoral thesis. The paper described the chemical structure of organic colloids—substances that spread throughout and combine with other structures, such as coal, and change the properties of these structures. Her work at the BCURA lab gave scientists a deeper knowledge of coal, and the research inspired her to write or contribute to five scientific papers. She would stay at the lab for two more years.

The war now over, people throughout Europe were on the move. Many refugees living in the United Kingdom returned to their homes on the continent. One of them was French refugee and Franklin's mentor Weill, who moved to Paris. She kept in contact with her friends and colleagues from Cambridge, and she would soon provide Franklin with an opportunity to continue her work in a new country and in a new language.

CHAPTER FIVE

WORKING IN PARIS

In 1947, Franklin traveled across the English Channel to France and a new life. The war was over, and France was rebuilding. Paris promised a young scientist adventures and challenges. Through Weill, Franklin had been offered a position at the Laboratoire Central des Services Chimiques de l'État. This research center began as a gunpowder lab for the French government. In 1947, it worked on peaceful, practical science. The lab's research was dedicated to the country's manufacturing industries. Discoveries made there allowed French inventors to develop new tools and machinery for the country's factories.

LIVING ON THE LEFT BANK

Franklin found an apartment on the top floor of a house on the Rue Garancière. The widow who owned the house had

At 27, Franklin moved to Paris to work at the Laboratoire Central des Services Chimiques de l'État.

strict rules for tenants. They could use the bathtub only once a week, and they could never make noise after 9:30 in the evening. Tenants could use the kitchen to make their meals, but they had to wait until the widow's maid finished preparing the widow's meal.

X Rays and Snowflakes

Although electron microscopes and other advanced optical gear can now peer into atom-sized structures, X-ray crystallography is still a useful method to analyze the atomic structure of various materials. When X rays bounce off a crystal, the light scatters them into clear patterns. The diffraction pattern can tell a researcher about a material's density and the arrangement of its elements and chemical bonds. The theory goes all the way back to the 1600s and the astronomer Johannes Kepler. Kepler theorized all snowflakes have different, but always six-sided, patterns because of the way water particles are packed when frozen. X rays provided proof of Kepler's idea. The bonds between hydrogen and oxygen in each molecule of water form a six-sided hexagon as the water freezes into the form of snow. Table salt—the first substance to be X-rayed for science—shows the same regular geometry, but it forms bonds in the shape of a cube.

The Seine River divides Paris into the Left Bank, which was Franklin's new neighborhood, and the Right Bank, where the lab was. On foot or using her bike, Franklin crossed the Seine each morning to the Right Bank. At the lab, she met Jacques Mering, an expert in X-ray crystallography. This difficult science would set Franklin on the path to her life's work and bring her fame as a scientist.

X–RAY DISCOVERIES

X rays are a spectrum of high-frequency radiation.

They are invisible to the naked eye. X rays can also penetrate materials such as wood or the skin and bones of an animal. X rays enable a doctor to examine a broken leg or the structure of a plant. When X rays are passed through a microscopic substance, such as the fiber of a cotton plant, they diffract, or break up, and form a pattern. Exposed to ordinary light, the pattern can then be printed on a photographic plate.

X-ray crystallography is a way of photographing things that cannot be seen. Diffraction patterns can reveal the chemical structure of substances that are too small to see through a microscope. By studying X-ray diffraction, skilled scientists can build a model of a tiny, invisible chemical molecule. This helps them understand how organisms, such as viruses and bacteria, are put together.

But the radiation from an X ray can be dangerous to anyone exposed to it for a long time, including researchers. X rays can affect the genes and chromosomes within a cell and cause defective cells to mutate and replicate themselves, resulting in cancer. As cancer

Science as Art

X-ray crystallography creates beautiful images of the intricate patterns found in the structures of different substances. X-ray crystallography was entering the art world while Franklin was working. At the 1951 Festival of Britain, designers offered a series of prints and lace based on X-ray images of insulin and hemoglobin. Today, art galleries and several websites offer framed X-ray diffraction images for sale.

cells take control of a body, healthy cells are crowded out. The affected person's health fails. Franklin may have known that X rays were dangerous, but she took few precautions in her laboratory. Instead, she attended the X-ray machinery and cameras for long hours.

COAL AND GRAPHITE

Working with Mering, Franklin used X-ray crystallography to examine two carbon-based compounds: coal and graphite, the material used to make pencil lead. The X-ray images she created revealed the chemical bonds that created certain properties, such as color, hardness, or absorbency—the ability to hold water.

Mering and Franklin studied different kinds of coal, placing the black rocks under high heat and pressure. Some coal samples turned to graphite under extreme conditions, although some did not. Using her background in chemistry and mathematics, and working carefully with cameras and X-ray generators, Franklin worked out why. She prepared coal samples and applied heat to bring the samples to a precise temperature. Once the camera took its picture, she measured the angles and distances in the structure of the image. She used complicated math formulas to work out the hidden structures.

The carbon crystals in some coals were strongly linked, whereas those in others had weaker links. When the links were weak, the carbon crystals broke down under high heat. Hard coal changed into softer graphite. But when the links were strong, coal was nongraphitizing, meaning it did not turn to graphite. Franklin isolated the nongraphitizing types of coal, which could be used to make useful products, such as tough glassware that did not break under high heat. In the Paris lab, she also came to realize that understanding coal was only one use for X-ray crystallography. X rays could create images of chemical molecules, the building blocks of life.

MOUNTAINEERING

There was more to life in France than lab work. Franklin left the city whenever she could to take long hikes in the mountains. She enjoyed the toughest, steepest, and most dangerous trails through the French Alps, which reach 15,500 feet (4,800 m).[1]

Back in the city, she enjoyed the company of her coworkers. On many days, the group ate together at Chez Solange, their favorite

In Honor of Rosalind Franklin

France has honored Franklin for the work she did with X-ray crystallography while in Paris. The country named a street, the Rue Rosalind Franklin, after her. It runs through the EDF laboratory complex at Paris-Saclay, 20 miles (32 km) south of the capital. In the United States, a private graduate school for medicine and science in North Chicago, Illinois, took the name Rosalind Franklin University.

restaurant. She made new friends and saw many old ones from the United Kingdom when they came to visit. She spoke French and loved visiting shops, where she would carry on long arguments with the owners.

For Franklin, arguing was a pleasant, interesting way to pass the time. In the lab or in a shop, she did not hesitate to give her opinion. If she thought a friend or a colleague was wrong about something important, she said so. She held her ground and did not back down. The Paris lab was often the scene of lively arguments, sometimes with voices raised. Many scientific questions were not settled, and everybody had their own opinions. An important part of life as a scientist is to form theories and opinions and then defend them against anyone who disagrees.

HOME TO THE UNITED KINGDOM

The work in the research laboratory was interesting, but the pay was modest. Franklin did not mind some hardships as long as she had interesting work to do and interesting people with whom to share her ideas. "I find life interesting," she wrote in a letter home. "I have good friends . . . and I find infinite kindness and good will among the people I work with. All that is far more important than a larger meat ration or more frequent baths."[2]

Hiking in the picturesque French Alps was one of Franklin's favorite pastimes.

SCIENCE
SPOTLIGHT

OSWALD AVERY EXPLORES DNA

For many years, scientists believed proteins in a cell carried genetic information. Proteins are much more complex molecules than DNA. Scientists thought that simple DNA molecules could not possibly carry the complex set of instructions needed to map out an organism.

That consensus began to change in the 1940s through a series of clever experiments. Oswald Avery was a researcher at the Rockefeller Institute for Medical Research in the United States. He cultured two different strains of pneumococcal bacteria. One strain was called S, for smooth coating, and the other R, for rough coating. Then, he injected mice with the two different live strains simultaneously. The S strain disguised itself from the immune defenses in the mice. This allowed the bacteria cells to multiply and eventually kill the mice. The R strain did not disguise itself. The mice immune systems attacked R-strain cells, and the bacteria did no harm.

Avery injected mice with the two different strains once more. But this time, instead of live S-strain bacteria, he used dead S bacteria and live R bacteria. Surprisingly, the mice died, despite the S strain being dead. Somehow, the R bacteria, which had not affected the mice in the first experiment, had taken on the characteristics of the fatal S strain. Avery started to hunt for the genetic changes that caused the switch. He isolated every element of the bacteria's cell structure, eliminating them all until only one remained: DNA. His conclusion was that DNA must be the part of the cell that carries inherited traits.

Avery at work in his lab

But the United Kingdom was still home and where friends and family lived. Franklin hoped for an opportunity to return, but she wanted to carry on her work in X-ray crystallography. When meeting scientists from the United Kingdom, she asked about work going on in the field. From Charles Coulson, a physicist, she learned about the interesting work going on at a laboratory at King's College in London. The scientists at King's College were using X-ray crystallography to examine large biological molecules. They were studying proteins and DNA.

In 1950, she applied for a fellowship. By that time, Franklin's fame had grown. She was giving lectures and publishing papers in scientific journals. She won the fellowship and returned to England to start work at King's College in January 1951.

AT THE KING'S COLLEGE LAB

U pon returning to the United Kingdom, Franklin began new work in biophysics at King's College. She moved into a new home in London's South Kensington neighborhood. She also had a new field of research. She was to apply her knowledge of X-ray crystallography to DNA.

This mysterious chemical is present in everything that lives. Humans, cats, birds, trees, bacteria, and viruses all have long strands of DNA contained in chromosomes, structures present in the nucleus in every single cell. DNA exists only in living cells. There is no DNA in rocks, sand, or gold, or in gases such as carbon dioxide. It seemed logical to these researchers that DNA must have something to do with life. But what?

Franklin started work at the laboratory at King's College in January 1951.

Chemists divide the many compounds formed by the elements into two main groups: acids and bases. In 1929, researchers discovered the DNA molecule contained four different chemical bases, now called nucleobases: adenine, guanine, thymine, and cytosine. Their next step was figuring out how the four bases combined to create the vast storehouse of information that created living organisms.

Researchers believed this process might have something to do with the thousands of DNA segments, also known as genes, found in each chromosome. To scientists studying heredity, it seemed possible that DNA provided the instruction set that determined inherited traits: height, skin color, the color of eyes and hair, the shape of a nose, or an inherited disease, such as hemophilia.

But how could it possibly work? The human body is incredibly complex, but DNA is quite simple, chemically speaking. It consists of only a few elements and compounds linked together by ordinary chemical bonds. How could such a simple molecule carry

A Book Inspires the Hunt for DNA

Many of the scientists working on DNA, including Watson and Crick, took inspiration from the same short book. *What Is Life?* was written by Erwin Schrödinger and published in 1944. In the book, Schrödinger claimed chromosomes must be the carriers of genetic information. He also challenged the scientific world to analyze the molecules found within chromosomes, uncover how they worked, and learn how they replicated themselves. It was only logical, Schrödinger claimed, that chromosomes must duplicate whenever cells divide—but how?

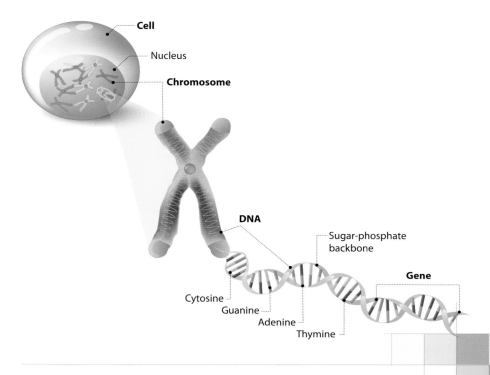

Cell

Nucleus

Chromosome

DNA

Sugar-phosphate backbone

Gene

Cytosine

Guanine

Adenine

Thymine

Chromosomes in a cell's nucleus contain DNA.

the billions of instructions needed to create an individual, and how did it vary to generate so many different organisms?

NOT BEST FRIENDS

John Randall was head of the lab at King's College. He assigned Franklin her work, showed her around the lab, and gave her information on the equipment. There were X-ray machines, cameras, and devices for heating and mixing chemical samples. She would be free to design her own experiments and write her findings in papers and journal articles. She could even order new equipment, if she needed it. Randall also introduced her to her new colleague, Maurice Wilkins, who was investigating the structure and function of DNA.

On the first day they met, Wilkins thought Franklin was his new lab assistant. She quickly and firmly corrected this misunderstanding. Franklin, in fact, now had a capable assistant of her own: Raymond Gosling. He was a student at King's College who was working on a PhD degree. He was working on X-ray diffraction research with Wilkins, and he had already discovered DNA had a crystalline structure. With Franklin's help, Gosling would make progress toward his degree.

Wilkins was a quiet, thoughtful man. He had been at King's for several years and had made many friends while working on DNA. With Franklin, he now shared a simple goal:

Raymond Gosling

Born in 1926 in Wembley, England, Gosling studied physics at University College, London, graduating in 1947. He then joined Randall's King's College research lab, where Randall assigned him to assist Maurice Wilkins with his work on DNA research. Randall later assigned Gosling to work with the new arrival, Rosalind Franklin, creating one of many sources of tension between Franklin and Wilkins.

Gosling also missed out on the fame offered to Watson and Crick for uncovering the secrets of DNA—even though it was Gosling who took the famous photograph that would be instrumental in decoding DNA's structure. Gosling moved away from DNA research in the 1960s. He became a professor of physics, working at the University of Saint Andrews in Scotland and the University of the West Indies in Jamaica. Later, he joined the medical school at Guy's Hospital in London. He died in 2015 at the age of 88.

Wilkins with a model of DNA in 1962

to understand the molecule's chemical structure and how it worked. At first, Franklin and Wilkins worked well together. Like any two scientists working on the same problem, they had some disagreements. Wilkins was not happy that Randall removed Gosling as Wilkins's assistant and assigned him to Franklin instead.

Unknown to Wilkins or Franklin, Randall was manipulating both of them. He encouraged competition between his researchers, even to the point of encouraging arguments among them. In Franklin's case, he had told her that eventually she would be the lead scientist on DNA and X-ray crystallography.

This led to a confrontation at a scientific conference in the summer of 1951, where Wilkins gave a talk on his progress. He reported that the X-ray images taken of DNA samples showed a clear central axis. This meant there was high probability that the molecule took the shape of a helix. He enjoyed a round of polite applause, walked from the lectern, and found himself facing Franklin, who told him he should go back to his microscopes and leave the X-ray crystallography to her.

From that day forward, Franklin and Wilkins could not get along. In addition to the professional rivalry, they were two very different people. Franklin enjoyed lively debate and did not mind an engaging argument. She had little patience for people she disagreed with or whom she found uninteresting. She cut people off, spoke over them, and raised her voice. When she believed she was right, she held her ground and fought to the end.

But Wilkins did not like disagreements of any sort. Franklin's quick temper put him on edge. Perhaps because she was a woman, Wilkins did not enjoy debating science with her, much less arguing. He found it hard to treat her as an equal. Another problem was Franklin's experience. Using X-ray diffraction, she had studied only coal, a nonliving substance. Wilkins did not believe she was qualified to carry out research on DNA.

ELECTRON MICROSCOPES

Today, scientists have much more powerful methods than X-ray crystallography to view the structure of different materials directly. The electron microscope uses a beam of electrons to explore a tiny world. These devices can magnify cells, molecules, bacteria, viruses, and other substances up to two million times larger than their actual sizes.[1]

The original transmission electron microscope, or TEM, has gone through several improvements since its invention in the 1930s. Modern devices can magnify specimens up to 50 million times, and they can distinguish objects as close together as 89 trillionths of a meter.[2] A newer version, known as a scanning electron microscope, uses an electron beam that creates an emission of particles from the surface of a sample. This creates three-dimensional images, allowing a researcher to see an object in much greater detail. Rendered on a computer screen, the image can be colorized or edited by a researcher to bring out important details and features.

Using an electron microscope, a doctor or scientist can examine individual cells or molecules. This is useful in the detection and treatment of diseases such as cancer. But unlike a conventional microscope, an electron microscope kills living organisms. In recent years, scientists and engineers have proposed a solution. A quantum

Electron microscopes are powerful machines that allow scientists to observe very tiny specimens.

electron microscope would be able to examine objects with an electron beam that does not interact with the sample. The concept relies on a startling phenomenon called quantum weirdness. The concept states that at the smallest-known scale of atomic structure, particles can act on each other at a distance without actually directly interacting. In theory, this principle could allow an electron probe to detect a sample without interacting with it, affecting it, or killing it.

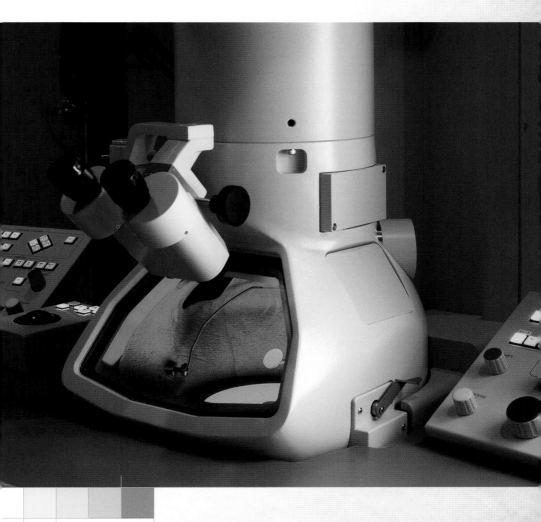

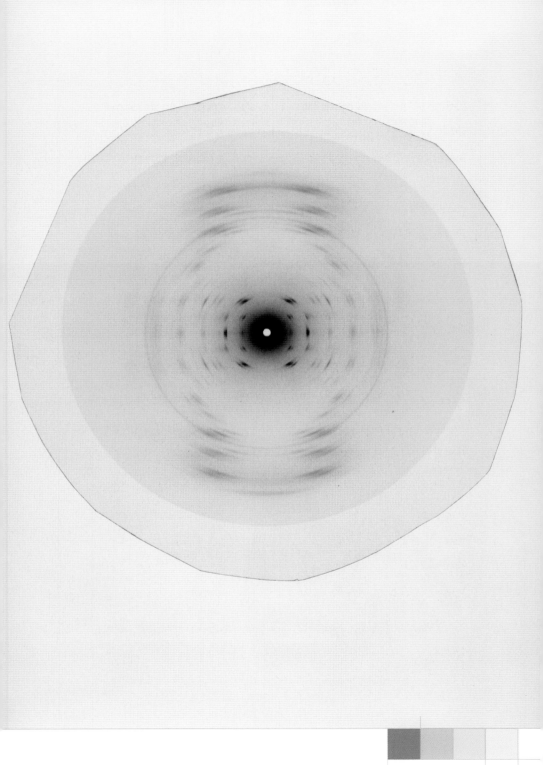

A MYSTERIOUS HELIX

Other scientists in other labs were also working on the same DNA problem. Linus Pauling was studying DNA at the California Institute of Technology. At Cambridge University, James Watson and Francis Crick were studying the molecule. The scientists raced to be the first with the answer. During the next two years, Franklin, Gosling, Wilkins, Pauling, Crick, and Watson all eagerly competed to solve the DNA puzzle.

At the King's College laboratory, Franklin and Gosling used an X-ray machine and a camera to take images of DNA samples. The diffraction of X-ray light revealed the molecule in three dimensions. There were blank spaces and dark spaces alternating on the diffraction images. The appearance and shape of the images suggested the form of a curving ladder: a helix. But the exact arrangement of its components remained invisible.

The scientists at King's College had worked out that DNA had a crystalline structure. The components were arranged in a repeating pattern. It seemed possible to understand the structure by mathematical calculation. Like Franklin and Gosling, Wilkins believed the structure might be a helix.

Franklin set to work. Her goal was to determine a precise, clear diffraction pattern. Using that pattern, it would be possible to understand the arrangement of chemical bases in DNA.

Wilkins produced this X-ray image of mouse DNA while at King's College.

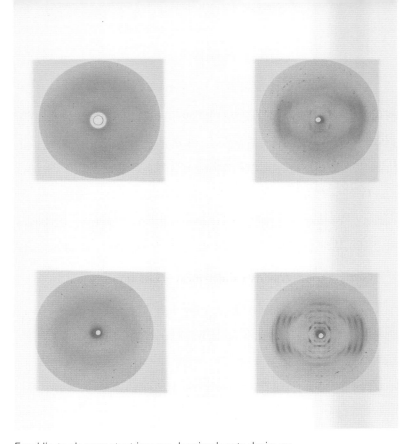

Franklin took many test images, honing her techniques.

It would take patience and careful adjustment of the X-ray cameras and instruments in the lab. Through the weeks of study, she discovered that DNA actually has two forms, which she named the A and B forms. In dry conditions, DNA tended to take on a hard crystalline structure: the A form. But in the presence of moisture or high humidity, DNA tended to the B form, bonding with the water molecules and forming long fibers rather than hard crystals. The fibers of B-form DNA created a clearer image of the molecule's structure than the crystalline structures of A-form DNA.

With Gosling assisting, Franklin took dozens of exposures, some of them lasting for days. Some images were clear, whereas others were not. For one particular photo, Gosling struggled for a long time with humidity. The water vapor swirling around the DNA fiber, coming from a narrow brass tube used in the experiment, made the image too blurry. Wilkins suggested Gosling wrap a piece of rubber around the tube.

Gosling tried Wilkins's suggestion. The humidity immediately dropped. This made the details clearer, sharper, and easier to measure. When Gosling photographed the fiber, a startlingly precise image emerged. Later, Franklin labeled it *Photograph 51*—an image that would inspire one of the most important scientific breakthroughs in history.

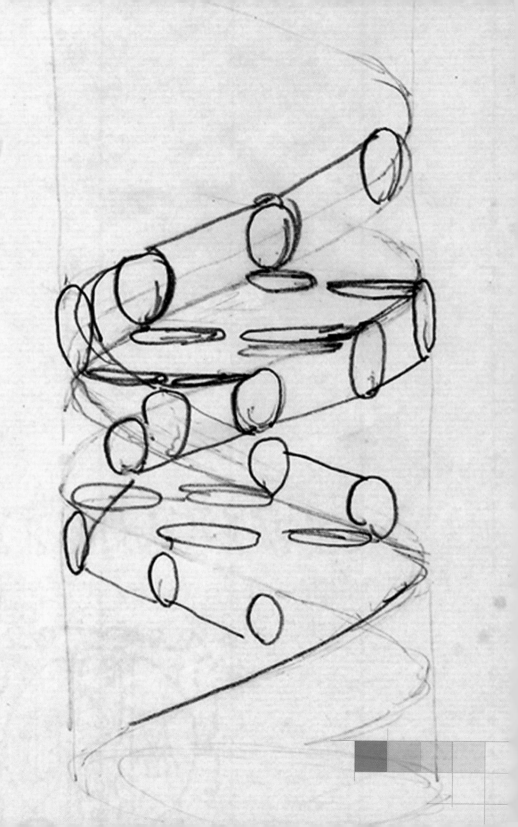

CHAPTER SEVEN

COMPETITION FROM CAMBRIDGE

W hile Franklin was using X-ray images to study the DNA molecule at King's College, Watson and Crick were working at the Cavendish Laboratory at Cambridge University. It was one of the world's most prestigious and respected research laboratories. Crick had become an expert in X-ray crystallography. Both men knew about Franklin's DNA studies at King's College, and both knew her colleague Wilkins.

Watson and Crick worked well together, although they had different personalities. Watson was studious, whereas Crick was more outgoing. At Cavendish, they were studying the three-dimensional structure of proteins. But the growing general opinion among experts in the field was that DNA held the secrets of inherited traits. It was this molecule, rather

Crick completed this early sketch of DNA's possible structure in 1953.

The Cavendish Laboratory Today

Founded in 1874, the Cavendish Laboratory at Cambridge University remains one of the leading research labs in the world. Now part of the university's department of physics, the lab carries out research in astrophysics, magnetism, quantum theory, microelectronics, medicine, and biology. In 2016, researchers at Cavendish invented a magnifying glass that can focus light down to the scale of single atoms. The device uses nanoparticles of gold to make a pico-cavity, a space that is as small as a single atom. This could allow scientists in the future to create new nanostructures. One possible technology is a data-storage device that would store information as molecular vibrations.

than proteins in cells, that caused traits to pass from one generation to the next. But how DNA functioned remained a mystery. The secret must be in its structure and chemical makeup—and it was this mystery that Wilkins, Watson, Crick, Franklin, Gosling, and Randall were now all trying to solve.

Through the years, Wilkins became close friends with Crick. The scientist from King's College enjoyed visiting Crick's lively home in Cambridge, where students, colleagues, and friends often gathered for conversation. During one discussion, the scientists came up with one possible way to understand DNA structure: building a three-dimensional model.

Wilkins had already suggested such a model to Franklin. He thought building and manipulating a physical model might yield better results than struggling through a lot of complex math. But Franklin disagreed. Without precise measurements, a model was only an educated guess. She wanted to have the answer worked out on paper, with the numbers and precise calculations giving the proof.

Their disagreement led to another argument, which built on the anger Wilkins had toward Randall's transfer of Gosling to become Franklin's assistant. Wilkins was not happy that Franklin now had use of the best camera equipment at the lab. Franklin was also secretive about her work with Gosling and their findings, a habit that Wilkins found irritating and unprofessional. Wilkins and Franklin no longer collaborated in the lab. Even though two of the best scientists at King's College were working on the same problem, they rarely spoke.

THE SEMINAR

On November 21, 1951, Franklin and other King's College scientists held a seminar to present their findings. In front of a small audience, which included Watson from Cavendish, Franklin revealed some interesting new facts about DNA. She shared her findings about the molecule's two forms, A and B. She described how DNA changes forms depending on the amount of water present. She had observed that the A form had a crystalline structure, whereas the B form included water molecules, which seemed to affect the structure of DNA.

The water in the B form of DNA appeared to bond with phosphate. This gave a clue to DNA's underlying structure.

James Watson

Arriving at the Cavendish Laboratory in 1951 was the turning point for James D. Watson. He was an American from Chicago, Illinois, a recent graduate of the University of Chicago and Indiana University. He collaborated with Francis Crick to study the structure of DNA at Cavendish. In 1956, he moved to the department of biology at Harvard University in Massachusetts, and in 1968 he was appointed director of the Cold Spring Harbor Laboratory in New York, where he researched cancer. Watson's career at Cold Spring came to an end in 2007. He retired after making controversial remarks indicating he believed race was a factor in an individual's intelligence.

Phosphate must be present somewhere in the strands of the molecule. But where was it, and how was it arranged?

A MISTAKEN DNA MODEL

Watson took what information he remembered on DNA structure from the seminar back to Cambridge. Though he was not absolutely clear on the details, he talked over the research with Crick. The two scientists set out to build their model. They used pieces of cardboard and bits of wire. The model showed the phosphates in three strands in the center of the molecule. The four nucleobases stretched out from the strands like branches from a tree.

Once they finished the work, they invited Wilkins and Franklin up to Cambridge to have a look. When she entered the Cambridge lab, Franklin took one look at the DNA model and immediately saw that it was all wrong. Watson and Crick had put the phosphate strands in the wrong place. Because water was present in the B form of DNA, the phosphates must be somewhere on the outside of the molecule, where they would be available to bond with the water. This structure would also prevent water from interfering with the function of the chemical bases inside the DNA molecule.

There was another error with Watson's and Crick's model. The phosphate strands had negative charges. They would repel one another other instead of attracting one another. It would be impossible for a molecule with such an arrangement to function at all. The molecule would fly apart. Watson and Crick realized Franklin was right, and they would have to try again. They had all the elements of DNA present, but the model's arrangement was wrong.

Franklin's visit to the Cavendish Laboratory caused a stir. She had a better command of the math and understanding of DNA's molecular structure than Watson or Crick. Lawrence Bragg, the head of the Cambridge lab, was losing patience with his team. He knew Wilkins and Franklin were hard at work on DNA

The Secret of Life on Display

London's Science Museum is a busy place. Crowds of schoolchildren rub elbows with thousands of tourists for a look at famous discoveries in astronomy, physics, biology, and chemistry. There are rockets, satellites, vehicles, and strange objects that are hard to describe. But one glass case draws a lot of curious visitors. Inside the case is a strange contraption of wire and thin, hexagon-shaped metal plates. This is a reconstruction of the original Watson and Crick model of DNA, shining under the museum's bright lights.

James Watson, *left*, and Francis Crick, *right*, with their DNA model in 1953

structure at King's College. They seemed to have a better handle on the subject than the Cambridge scientists did.

Bragg believed that it was not productive to have two important British labs competing on the same research. The war had ended only a few years before, and resources were scarce. Researchers should not be duplicating efforts. Bragg ordered Watson and Crick to stop working on DNA and focus their research on proteins. Franklin and Wilkins at King's College could move ahead with their work without interference or competition from Cambridge. Crick and Watson reluctantly agreed. They sent their DNA model down to King's College. But they kept in close contact with Wilkins.

Francis Crick

Francis Crick was born in England in 1916 and studied physics as an undergraduate. During World War II, he performed technical research on mine development. After the war, he focused his research on biology and earned his doctorate from Cambridge University in 1954. In 1962, Crick became head of Cambridge's molecular biology laboratory. He went on to write several popular books on science and died in 2004.

REVEALING DNA

At the Cavendish Laboratory, Watson was still reeling from the dressing down Franklin had given him and his DNA model. Although Bragg had stopped Watson's DNA work, Watson was determined to put his model back together. He knew he did not have much time.

In the meantime, Watson and Crick had a chance to meet and trade ideas with Erwin Chargaff at Cambridge. Chargaff had discovered that pairs of DNA bases always appear in equal proportions. But the conversation did not go well. Instead of trading ideas and debating theories, Watson took a personal dislike to Chargaff. He was a researcher working in the same field and thus Watson's competition—and Watson, as a result, wanted to downplay the Chargaff ratios in his own work.

Bragg with an electron microscope in 1942

MOVING ON

Meanwhile in London, Franklin was preparing to look for another position. She was unhappy at the King's College lab. She believed she could carry on her work at a different lab. She had experience, a doctorate, and the respect of other chemists and physicists in the United Kingdom. She had also developed great skill as an X-ray crystallographer. X-ray crystallography is demanding work. Creating an X-ray image of a tiny strand of fiber could take as long as 100 hours at a range as close as 15 millimeters.[1] The equipment had to be set up and operated with great care. And after the image was developed, Franklin's work was not done. She did not trust images alone to tell the whole story. She wanted to prove the findings with math before presenting any theories.

In her way of thinking, mathematics could provide the only proof of any scientific theory. She would not be ready to present any findings to the world until she made the numbers work.

DNA and Genes

Before the early 1950s, scientists could not conceive of how long the DNA molecule really is. When stretched to its full length, it is approximately 6 feet (1.8 m) long.[2] The molecule is carried on structures called chromosomes found in every cell. Human cells contain 23 pairs of chromosomes, but other species might have more or fewer pairs.[3] Three billion base pairs create approximately 30,000 separate human genes.[4] The entire complex of genes contained in chromosomes is known as a genome. Scientists at the Human Genome Project have mapped out the arrangement of genes on the genome, finishing the work in 2003.

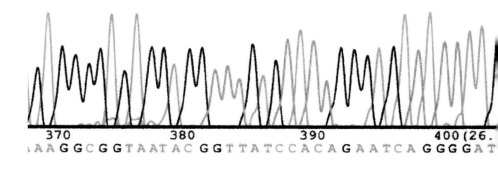

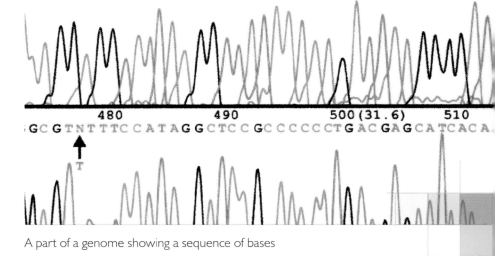

A part of a genome showing a sequence of bases

Competition from other scientists in the United Kingdom or abroad did not bother her. The race to publish in a scientific journal could lead to public embarrassment, as rival scientists pointed out mistakes and answered with their own theories. Franklin did not want to take that risk.

In 1952, Franklin took a holiday to climb the Italian Alps, visit the historic city of Venice in Italy, and tour the coast of Dalmatia, on the coast of the Adriatic Sea in Croatia. It was enjoyable

Fed Up at King's College

Franklin's decision to move from King's College to another lab was motivated by more than only research opportunities. She was having a difficult time working with her colleagues, who she believed were not up to the task of researching DNA. She revealed her thoughts in a letter to Adrienne Weill. "The other serious trouble is that there isn't a first-class or even a good brain among them," she wrote. "In fact nobody with whom I particularly want to discuss anything, scientific or otherwise, and I so much prefer to work under somebody who commands my respect and can offer some encouragement."[5]

to leave home, see foreign countries, appreciate the air and the mountains, and think about her future. She realized she was ready to leave King's College. When she returned to the United Kingdom, John Randall granted her permission to move to another important University of London research lab, Birkbeck. But first, she would wrap up some of her DNA research.

SCIENCE
SPOTLIGHT

THE HUMAN GENOME PROJECT

There are approximately 30,000 genes in humans, each of them consisting of long sequences of DNA, and each containing a pattern of chemical base pairs, approximately three billion in all.[6] The precise pattern of base pairs is unique to each individual. After Franklin and her fellow English researchers determined that DNA was the key to heredity, a new challenge was set out for scientists: mapping out all the genes on the entire human genome.

The work began in 1990 in the US Department of Energy and the National Institutes of Health, where Watson was the director of the project. Although the goal was to have the project complete within 15 years, the human genome was completely mapped by April 2003, beating the deadline by two years. Unlike many high-level government projects, there was no secrecy involved in the Human Genome Project. The complete genetic map of humans is available to anyone who can access GenBank, a database available on the Internet.

What to do with all this information? Medical researchers can trace the origins of a cancer cell down to its genes and discover how they interact with normal cells in the human body. Biologists can study the genome to understand how variations and mutations can lead to evolutionary adaptations, in humans and other species. Genetic modification is also leading to the creation of new strains of seeds and plants. The science of GMOs—genetically modified organisms—is controversial among those who believe such manipulation can harm those who consume new species of grains, vegetables, fruits, and animals.

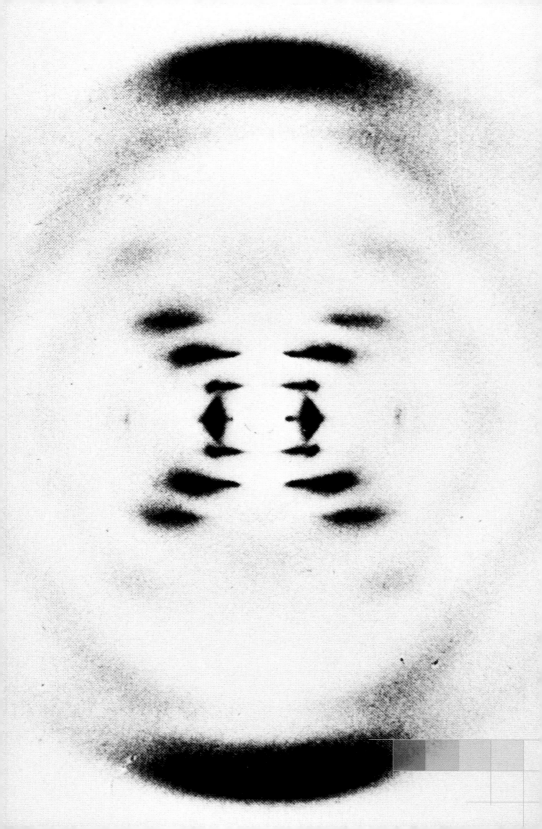

CHAPTER NINE

DOING THE MATH

As Watson and Crick returned to their three-dimensional model, Franklin and Gosling were trying a new two-dimensional approach to mapping DNA's structure. The key to their research was the Patterson function. This formula used measurements taken directly from the patterns on the X-ray images. The shadows of these patterns changed, and this change could be measured. The darker the spot, the higher a concentration of a certain chemical. Franklin believed the data she took from the images would eventually reveal the underlying structure of the DNA molecule.

But Franklin and Gosling had no computers to perform their calculations. They had to do all of the advanced math by hand with a pencil, eraser, paper, and simple calculating machine.

An X-ray diffraction image of the B form of DNA from Franklin's lab, 1953

The work went on for weeks, through hundreds of pages. But Franklin forged ahead, believing that A and B forms of DNA might have different basic structures. Before publishing anything, she wanted to fully understand their structures. In her opinion, honest science lay in the numbers and mathematical proof, not in a collection of cardboard cutouts strung together with wire.

Other scientists at King's College asked Franklin about her work. After all, they were all supposed to be working together. But her fellow scientists were also her competitors, so Franklin kept her notebooks well guarded. She was not ready to announce any findings, publish any articles, or even talk much about what she was doing. She was also highly suspicious of the friendships between researchers at King's College and Cambridge University. She may have believed Wilkins was leaking her data to Watson and Crick.

In February 1953, Franklin had an important mathematical breakthrough. Using the Patterson function, she worked out DNA's double helix structure. The base pairs on each strand of the molecule and the complementary way they were positioned allowed the molecule to replicate itself, making an exact copy every time it divided. Franklin did the math—the possible combinations of these bases were infinite. The incredibly long DNA ladder could, in theory, hold millions of steps. This fact was central to the variety of life-forms that arise from DNA.

Meanwhile, at Cambridge, Watson and Crick were nearly done with their physical model. Bragg granted them permission to publish their findings. In the race to understand DNA, the Cavendish Laboratory would win this round. Using Franklin's data and the clues provided by *Photograph 51*, they drafted a short article for the April 1953 issue of *Nature*, a prestigious scientific journal.

Proving the Model

For many years after the Watson-Crick discovery of DNA structure, their double helix idea remained unproven. It was a convincing model, fitting all of DNA's properties and functions. But there was no way for scientists to look directly at the DNA molecule and confirm it. For the rest of her life, Franklin and many other scientists treated the model as a theory—an idea yet to be reliably tested. This changed in the late 1970s, when scientists succeeded in crystallizing DNA. This allowed them to examine the molecule's structure directly. In 1982, scientists proved Watson and Crick were correct.

The editors titled the article "Molecular Structure of Nucleic Acids." The authors briefly mentioned Wilkins and Franklin in the article's last paragraph: "We have also been stimulated by a knowledge of the general nature of the unpublished experimental results and ideas of Dr. M.H.F. Wilkins, Dr. R.E. Franklin and their co-workers at King's College, London."[1]

However, there was no mention in this important article of *Photograph 51*, nor of the details of the experimental work carried out at King's College. But *Nature* did publish an article by

Franklin and Gosling in the same issue. This article, "Molecular Configuration in Sodium Thymonucleate," went into detail about the A and B forms of DNA, and it also stated: "While the X-ray evidence cannot, at present, be taken as direct proof that the structure is helical, other considerations discussed below make the existence of a helical structure highly probable."[2]

A Journal of Science

Watson and Crick had good reason to present their DNA model in the science journal *Nature*. This British publication has been the leading journal of science research since it was first published in 1869. For prominent scientists, having an article published in *Nature* is a very important achievement. Many employers decide whom to hire based on articles published in *Nature* and other journals. Journals such as *Nature* pride themselves on the fact that articles are peer reviewed. Before publication, the articles are sent around to leading scientists in the field who probe for errors, misstatements, and other problems. Although peer-reviewed articles are standard in science, this test did not apply to Watson and Crick's DNA piece. Instead, believing that the data were self-evidently correct, *Nature* editors did not bother to send it out for review.

For Franklin, a picture simply was not sufficient—although it could show probability. In her view, nothing was yet proven until it could be shown through irrefutable evidence, and such was the nature of scientific research. As a result of their *Nature* article, Watson and Crick won credit as the scientists who discovered the double helix structure of DNA, whereas Franklin became a footnote. Watson and Crick took pride in their claim to be the first to fully understand DNA structure.

The scientific world took some interest in the articles, although for many others besides Franklin, the Watson-Crick model was still only that: a model, and therefore unproven.

The importance of the finding dawned on the scientific world only gradually in the decades to come. If the DNA molecule could be thoroughly analyzed, then science could track the genetic basis for a wide variety of physical characteristics, including inherited diseases. Each individual (except for identical twins) has a unique DNA pattern, one that no other organism on Earth has. This makes it possible to identify individuals by their DNA, which can be drawn from any of their body's cells, including cells from the skin, hair, tears, blood, sweat, and saliva. The Watson and Crick model opened up an entirely new field of science applicable to medicine, genetic studies, and even criminal investigations.

MOVING TO BIRKBECK

By the time the *Nature* articles appeared, Franklin had left King's College for her position at Birkbeck. She was no longer working on DNA. John Desmond Bernal, an expert in X-ray analysis, headed the Birkbeck lab. He believed Franklin would make a fine addition to the lab's work and boost its prestige. Franklin, for her part, greatly respected Bernal and was eager to work with him.

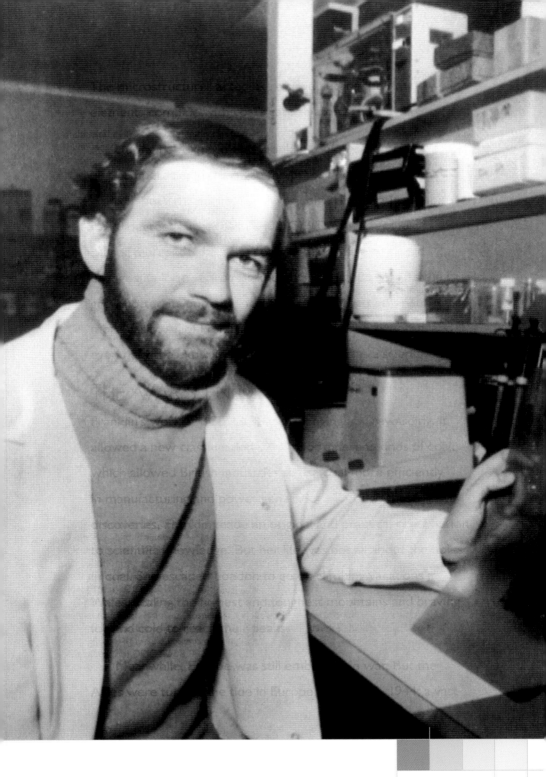

She started at Birkbeck in March 1953. But there were conditions on her move, laid down by Randall. First and foremost, she had to stop working on DNA. Nor could she publish any more papers on the subject. The King's lab had the privilege of DNA studies, and for anyone at Birkbeck, the subject would be out of bounds. Franklin still believed DNA structure was an unsolved problem. But she was happy to give up the King's College research for Birkbeck.

Franklin's work paved the way for future DNA discoveries, including Sir Alec Jeffreys's invention of DNA fingerprinting in 1984, a useful tool in medicine and criminal investigations.

CHAPTER
TEN

TO THE NEW WORLD

F ounded in 1823, Birkbeck offered night classes to students holding regular jobs. Its buildings were in the Bloomsbury neighborhood, where a set of old private houses contained the research labs. The rooms here were small and poorly ventilated. The office assigned to Franklin was up a narrow staircase to a former maid's room, although her X-ray equipment and cameras were down in the basement.

Her new research was on the tobacco mosaic virus (TMV). When a tobacco plant becomes infected with TMV, its leaves grow mottled and often yellow and curl before dying. The effects of TMV vary with the age of the plant, the conditions under which the plant grows, and the strain of TMV that causes

Rosalind Franklin in 1956, two years before her death

the symptoms. In addition to tobacco, the virus can affect valuable food plants, such as tomatoes.

The tobacco mosaic virus was the first virus to be discovered. Since its discovery in the nineteenth century, scientists have studied TMV to understand how viruses replicate, attach themselves to hosts, and travel from one organism to the next. The key to understanding the virus was to unlock its genetic code. Franklin created X-ray images to study the chemical makeup of the virus. Though the conditions of her leaving King's College required her to stop working on DNA, Franklin ignored this directive. She continued using X-ray analysis into the virus's genetics as part of her research into TMV.

Franklin saw an opportunity to apply her knowledge of TMV to medical research. She planned a project to examine the polio virus and its genetic structure. Poliomyelitis, a serious disease caused by the polio virus, was affecting hundreds of thousands of people every year. It was especially common among children. In 1953, the American researcher Jonas Salk introduced a vaccine, but Franklin and other researchers continued to study the virus's structure. She would secure important funding for her polio team in 1957.

The tobacco mosaic virus contains a long strand of genetic material.

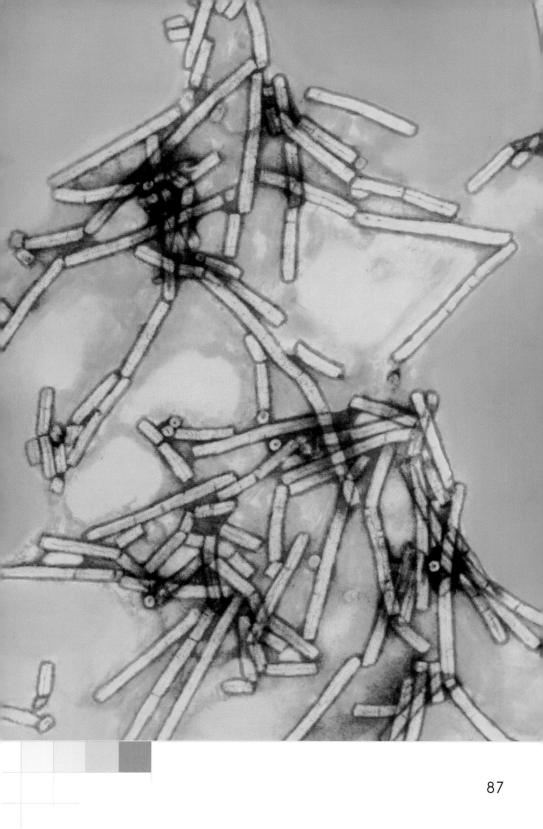

VISITING THE UNITED STATES

Meanwhile, Franklin's name and fame as an important researcher were spreading across the Atlantic Ocean. Her *Nature* article introduced her to many scientists who had never heard of her before. In the summer of 1954, she happily accepted an invitation to travel to the United States to attend a series of conferences on coal. Travel was one of her favorite things, and this would be her first time on a different continent.

When Franklin visited the Massachusetts Institute of Technology, Helen Watson, *right*, was studying radioactivity there during a time when few American scientists were women.

In 1954, air travel across the ocean was a complicated business. Franklin made stops at Reykjavik, Iceland, and Gander Airport in Newfoundland, Canada, before landing in Boston, Massachusetts. She visited cities and sites throughout the United States, including the University of Wisconsin–Madison; the Marine Biological Laboratory and Massachusetts Institute of Technology in Massachusetts; the University of California, Los Angeles; and the California Institute of Technology in Pasadena, California. Along the way, she offered lectures at universities and research labs on X-ray crystallography and her study of the tobacco mosaic virus. There were many striking differences between the United Kingdom and the United States. An enthusiastic mountaineer and hiker, Franklin enjoyed the vast open spaces, especially in the mountains of the American West, which poses such a contrast to the green British countryside. Another plus was the weather. California and other states enjoy more sunshine and clear days than foggy, cloudy, and rainy London.

Credit Where Credit Is Due

In October 1954, Crick made amends for the important oversight of not mentioning Gosling and Franklin's inspiring image of the DNA molecule. The magazine *Scientific American* published an article he wrote that acknowledged Franklin's contribution to his DNA research. The article featured *Photograph 51* and mentioned Rosalind Franklin as the creator of the image.

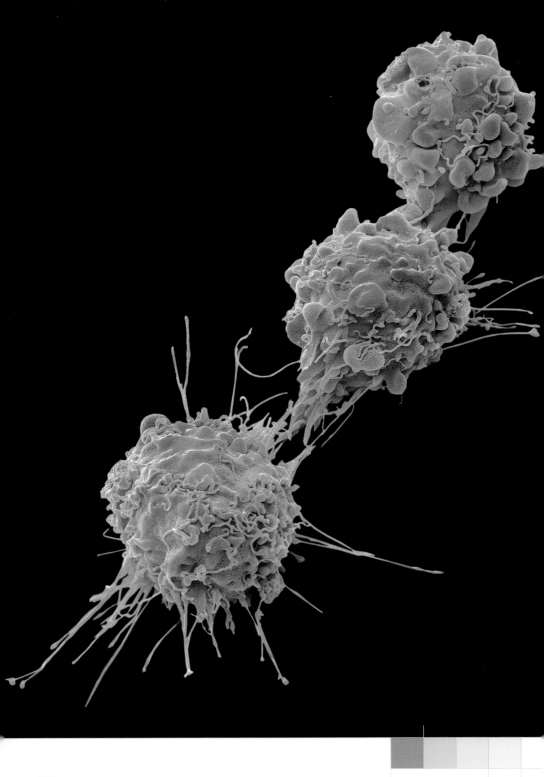

DIAGNOSIS: CANCER

Franklin returned to the United Kingdom later that year, but she took a second journey to the United States in 1956. During this journey, she came down with abdominal pains. The doctors she visited could not give her a diagnosis. Not wanting to interrupt her trip, she delayed her return to the United Kingdom. Meanwhile, Franklin suffered a strange pain that seemed to come and go without any cause. When she finally reached London in August 1956, the doctors gave her some bad news. There were two large lumps in her pelvis. They were cancerous tumors. Franklin was suffering from ovarian cancer.

The usual treatment for cancer in the 1950s was surgery to remove the cancer cells from the body. On September 4, Franklin underwent an operation. During the operation, Franklin's surgeons found the two tumors. Suspecting they had not found all of the cancer, they recommended another operation to remove her uterus. The operation meant that even if she survived the cancer, she would not be able to have children. Franklin consented to the second operation.

After the second operation, Franklin and her doctors believed all of the cancerous tumors had been removed. But they were aware that such an operation was not necessarily the end of the disease. Instead, the cancer could reappear and metastasize, or spread to other body organs.

Ovarian cancer cells as seen with an electron microscope

After her operations, Franklin still suffered symptoms, including pain and bleeding. When she returned to the doctors for another examination, they found a new tumor. Instead of more operations, however, doctors tried a new treatment. They prescribed a course of cobalt radiotherapy. In this treatment, the patient lay on a table while doctors operated a large machine. The machine produced gamma rays, which the operator directed at the tumor site. The radiation was intended to kill the cancer tissue, though it could also damage healthy tissue.

Although the treatments left her feeling weak and ill, Franklin continued her work. She was now considered a leader in the field of X-ray crystallography. She continued to publish papers in leading science journals. Foreign research labs, including the Sloan-Kettering Institute for Cancer Research in New York, sent her specimens for X-ray analysis. She was also working on models of TMV for the Brussels World's Fair. Though she had disdained building models while at King's College, she realized a three-dimensional model could help improve the public's understanding of chemistry and viruses.

The cause of Franklin's own illness, however, was still a mystery. Medical science could not yet explain why some people contracted cancers, whereas others remained cancer free. Later, scientists theorized that there might be genetic as well as environmental factors. There was cancer in Franklin's family, and the genes she received from her parents—the vast DNA code that provided the map in each of her body's cells—may have made her vulnerable to the disease.

The other factor could have been environmental. Franklin spent years working with X-ray generators that produced cancer-causing radiation. These instruments had to be precisely adjusted, carefully operated, and repaired. That meant standing near, and sometimes directly in the path of, harmful X-ray radiation.

No Nobel

For their discoveries of DNA structure, Crick and Watson, along with Wilkins, were awarded the Nobel Prize in Physiology or Medicine in 1962. The Nobel Prize is the most prestigious award in science. The Nobel is only awarded to living scientists. Had she lived, Franklin may have qualified to share the prize. The United Kingdom's Royal Society honored Franklin in another way. It created the Rosalind Franklin Award for women doing important work in the fields of science, technology, engineering, and mathematics. The winner receives a grant of £30,000 to continue her work and raise the profile of women scientists in the field.[1] In 2016, the winner was Professor Jo Dunkley of the University of Oxford, who studies astrophysics.

But the link between X rays and cancer was not well understood in the 1950s. Some scientists, as well as doctors operating X-ray equipment, had protection available, but they did not always bother to use it. Heavy lead aprons, for example, would have blocked the radiation. But in a research lab, where Franklin and her colleagues had to constantly move from place to place, putting on and taking off protective equipment was awkward. She frequently did not bother with it.

THE LAST YEAR

After her move to Birkbeck, Franklin remained friends with other DNA researchers, including Crick. She wrote often to Crick, whose renown among scientists was also growing. In early 1958, Crick was nominated to join the Royal Society, a prestigious group of leading researchers. Crick, as well as Watson, would become fellows of the society in 1959.

In the meantime, Franklin went into a serious physical decline. In early 1958, she was losing weight and growing weaker. One day, she found she could not use one of her arms. She was not immediately certain her cancer was to blame. It may have resulted from her work in the lab on the polio virus. She had declined to be immunized against the virus despite her close work with it.

By April 1958, Franklin lay dying in Royal Marsden Hospital in London. The doctors had tried another operation, but it failed to improve her condition. The Brussels World's Fair was in full swing, with her TMV model on display to general acclaim. Science and research took a leading place among the fair's exhibits. As fairgoers visited her work on display, Franklin's health took a turn for the worse. On the afternoon

In 2015, Franklin's life story and accomplishments were turned into a play.

of April 16, 1958, Rosalind Franklin died. She was 37 years old. Obituaries ran in the *New York Times*, the *Times* of London, and *Nature*. Members of her family were slightly taken aback at the international notice. Even after these many years, they understood very little of her work. Franklin believed that explaining it to them would not have been easy. But it was harder to confront the attitude of fellow researchers, some of whom did not accept that a woman could show as much or more insight and understanding as men in the field.

Watson, for one, never quite took Franklin seriously. From the time they were first acquainted, his main interests seemed to be her clothes, hair, and status as single or married. He enjoyed calling her "Rosy," a nickname she despised, and in *The*

Double Helix, his best-selling book about the many discoveries of DNA, he gave her only a few brief mentions.

But Franklin was not forgotten in the years that followed her death. Though the Nobel Prize eluded her, her fame as a DNA researcher has spread with the knowledge of DNA itself as the key to life and to genetics. As the many applications of this knowledge increase—reaching to medicine, human engineering, even the cloning of organisms—her contribution has been recognized by journal articles, scientific papers, and books. Franklin has had a prestigious British science award named in her honor, and she remains a leading symbol of the often neglected contributions of women to scientific knowledge.

Franklin's work paved the way for other young women to study science.

TIMELINE

1920
Rosalind Franklin is born in London, England, on July 25.

1938
Rosalind graduates from Saint Paul's Girls' School in London.

1941
Franklin completes undergraduate courses at Cambridge University.

1942
Franklin begins work for the British Coal Utilisation Research Association.

1945
Franklin earns her doctoral degree from Cambridge University.

1947
In February, Franklin moves to Paris, France, to take a position at the Laboratoire Central des Services Chimiques de l'État.

1950
Franklin applies for and wins a research fellowship at King's College to study DNA through X-ray crystallography.

1951

In November, with Watson in the audience, Franklin speaks at a seminar and describes DNA findings from X-ray crystallography; Watson and Crick begin building three-dimensional models of DNA.

1952

Franklin and her research assistant Raymond Gosling take *Photograph 51*, capturing an image of the helical structure of DNA.

1953

In February, Franklin completes data analysis of DNA's form, working out the molecule's double helix structure; in March, Franklin moves to the Birkbeck Laboratory in London to study tobacco mosaic virus; in April, *Nature* publishes Watson and Crick's article on DNA's structure as well as Franklin and Gosling's article on the A and B forms of DNA.

1954

Franklin takes her first trip to the United States.

1956

On Franklin's second trip to the United States, she experiences symptoms of cancer.

1958

Franklin dies of ovarian cancer on April 16 at age 37.

ESSENTIAL
FACTS

DATE OF BIRTH
July 25, 1920

PLACE OF BIRTH
London, England

DATE OF DEATH
April 16, 1958

PARENTS
Ellis and Muriel Franklin

EDUCATION
Saint Paul's Girls' School
Newnham College, Cambridge University

CAREER HIGHLIGHTS
- Early in her career, Franklin investigated how microstructures affected the porosity of coal at the British Coal Utilisation Research Association.
- She explored DNA structure through X-ray crystallography at King's College, eventually contributing to the discovery of the DNA double helix in 1953, though her work went unrecognized at the time.
- Late in her career, Franklin researched the tobacco mosaic virus at Birkbeck College, London, as well as the polio virus.

SOCIETAL CONTRIBUTIONS

- Franklin played a key role in uncovering the structure of DNA, the molecule that transmits genetic information from parents to offspring.
- Franklin was one of the only female researchers in her field at the time, and her work has inspired more women to pursue careers in science.

CONFLICTS

- Franklin was a demanding and often confrontational researcher. She had little patience for those she considered less able and did not like pursuing experiments that would not provide evidence to prove a theory.
- Franklin's long-running argument with Maurice Wilkins at King's College prevented the two from working together productively.

QUOTE

"It's very pretty, but how are they going to prove it?"
—*Rosalind Franklin commenting on Watson and Crick's model of DNA in 1953*

GLOSSARY

bond
The attractive force between different atoms that produces elements and more complex molecules.

chromosome
The carrier of genetic information found in every living cell.

diffraction
The scattering of X rays when passed through a material, creating a pattern that can reveal clues about the substance's molecular structure.

doctorate
The highest academic degree, also known as a PhD, allowing the holder the title of "doctor."

exposure
The action of allowing light to enter a camera, creating a photograph.

fellowship
A monetary award that allows a researcher to work at a scientific or academic institution.

gene
A unit of hereditary information found in a chromosome.

molecule
A structure of atoms and their bonds that creates the smallest unit of a chemical substance.

nanoparticle
A microscopic particle that is measured in billionths of a meter.

Patterson function
A math calculation that uses the darkness or lightness of image areas to provide information on density and chemical makeup.

protein
An amino acid chain present in organic material, such as skin, hair, or blood.

seminar
A meeting at which teachers, students, and researchers gather to discuss problems and breakthroughs in their field.

virus
A microscopic particle coated in protein that can reproduce only by infecting another organism and hijacking cells within that organism.

ADDITIONAL
RESOURCES

SELECTED BIBLIOGRAPHY

Glynn, Jenifer. *My Sister Rosalind Franklin: A Family Memoir.* London: Oxford UP, 2012. Print.

Maddox, Brenda. *Rosalind Franklin: The Dark Lady of DNA.* New York: Harper, 2002. Print.

Sayre, Anne. *Rosalind Franklin and DNA.* New York: Norton, 2000. Print.

Watson, James D. *DNA: The Secret of Life.* New York: Random, 2003. Print.

FURTHER READINGS

Lokere, Jillian. *Genetics: Unlocking the Secrets of Life.* Minneapolis: Abdo, 2015. Print.

Mooney, Carla. *Genetics: Breaking the Code of Your DNA.* White River Junction, VT: Nomad, 2014. Print.

WEBSITES

To learn more about Women in Science, visit **abdobooklinks.com**. These links are routinely monitored and updated to provide the most current information available.

FOR MORE INFORMATION

For more information on this subject, contact or visit the following organizations:

Dolan DNA Learning Center
334 Main Street
Cold Spring Harbor, NY 11724
516-367-5170
https://www.dnalc.org/about/directions.html#dolan
This facility on Long Island, New York, is part of the famous Cold Spring Harbor Laboratory, one of the world's leading research institutes. A hands-on science center, it allows students and visitors to explore current DNA research and investigative techniques. There are three laboratory classrooms, an auditorium, and 2,000 square feet of exhibition space.

The Field Museum/Pritzker Laboratory
1400 S. Lake Shore Drive
Chicago, IL 60605
312-922-9410
https://www.fieldmuseum.org/visit
A working DNA research laboratory with a viewing area for visitors and working scientists on hand to explain the work and answer questions.

University of Cambridge/Cavendish Laboratory
19 J J Thomson Avenue
Cambridge, England CB3 0HE
44-1223-337200
http://www.phy.cam.ac.uk/outreach/museum
The lab where Watson and Crick built their three-dimensional DNA model has a museum that is open to visitors. The museum offers a display of historical scientific equipment and exhibits on its breakthrough discoveries in astronomy, physics, and biology.

SOURCE
NOTES

CHAPTER 1. *PHOTOGRAPH 51*
None.

CHAPTER 2. GROWING UP SMART
1. Brenda Maddox. *Rosalind Franklin: The Dark Lady of DNA*. New York: Harper, 2002. Print. 41.

CHAPTER 3. WAR YEARS
1. Jenifer Glynn. *My Sister Rosalind Franklin: A Family Memoir*. Oxford: Oxford UP, 2012. Print. 60.

2. Brenda Maddox. *Rosalind Franklin: The Dark Lady of DNA*. New York: Harper, 2002. Print. 76.

CHAPTER 4. STUDYING THE HOLES IN COAL
1. Dr. Martin Johnes. "The Coal Industry in Wartime." *Wales History*. BBC, 2014. Web. 16 Jan. 2017.

2. Peter J. F. Harris, "Rosalind Franklin's Work on Coal, Carbon and Graphite." *Interdisciplinary Science Reviews* 26.3 (2001): 206. *University of Reading*. Web. 16 Jan. 2017.

CHAPTER 5. WORKING IN PARIS

1. "Mont Blanc." *Encyclopaedia Britannica*. Encyclopaedia Britannica, 4 Aug. 2011. Web. 16 Jan. 2017.

2. Jenifer Glynn. "Rosalind Franklin: The Not-So-Dark Lady of DNA." *OUPblog*. Oxford UP, 25 July 2012. Web. 16 Jan. 2017.

CHAPTER 6. AT THE KING'S COLLEGE LAB

1. "What Is Microscopy?" *John Innes Center*. John Innes Center, n.d. Web. 16 Jan. 2017.

2. Ibid.

CHAPTER 7. COMPETITION FROM CAMBRIDGE

None.

CHAPTER 8. REVEALING DNA

1. Brenda Maddox. *Rosalind Franklin: The Dark Lady of DNA*. New York: Harper, 2002. Print. 177.

2. "During Our Discussions on Genetics and DNA, I Recalled That the Amount of DNA in a Human Is Quite Substantial. . . ." *UCSB ScienceLine*. The Regents of the University of California, 2015. Web. 16 Jan. 2017.

3. "The Human Genome Project Completion: Frequently Asked Questions." *National Human Genome Research Institute*. Human Genome Project, 30 Oct. 2010. Web. 16 Jan. 2017.

4. Ibid.

5. Brenda Maddox. *Rosalind Franklin: The Dark Lady of DNA*. New York: Harper, 2002. Print. 172.

6. "An Overview of the Human Genome Project." *National Human Genome Research Institute*. Human Genome Project, 11 May 2016. Web. 16 Jan. 2017.

CHAPTER 9. DOING THE MATH

1. J. D. Watson and F. H. C. Crick. "Molecular Structure of Nucleic Acids: A Structure for Deoxyribose Nucleic Acid." *Nature* 4356 (25 Apr. 1953): 737. *Genome.gov*. Web. 16 Jan. 2017.

2. Rosalind E. Franklin and R. G. Gosling. "Molecular Configuration in Sodium Thymonucleate." *Nature* 4356 (25 Apr. 1953): 740–741. *Nature.com*. Web. 16 Jan. 2017.

CHAPTER 10. TO THE NEW WORLD

1. "Royal Society Rosalind Franklin Award and Lecture." *Royal Society*. Royal Society, 2017. Web. 16 Jan. 2017.

INDEX

ABOUT THE
AUTHOR

Tom Streissguth is the author of more than 100 books of nonfiction for the school and library market and the founder of the Archive of American Journalism, a unique collection of historical journalism that is presenting long-neglected work of major American authors including Jack London, Stephen Crane, Lincoln Steffens, Nellie Bly, and Ambrose Bierce. He currently lives in Woodbury, Minnesota.